THANK YOU
for teaching me

No part of this book may be scanned, reproduced or distributed in any printed or electronic form without the prior permission of the author or publisher.

Teachers Name _____

Student Name _____

Class Name _____

Grade Level _____

Number Of Students _____

"A Teacher affects eternity: he can never tell where his influence stops" - Henry Adams

 Class Photo

I would like to say thank you for....

_____

_____

_____

_____

_____

My Favorite memory......

_____

_____

_____

_____

_____

Something I learned about you………
_____
_____
_____
_____

Something I learned about myself……
_____
_____
_____
_____

Our class loved it when.....

My Favorite excursion....

_____

_____

_____

_____

My favorite part of our school day......

_____

_____

_____

_____

 I have learned..............

_____

_____

_____

_____

Now I look forward to...........

_____

_____

_____

_____

My Favorite Day.......

_____

_____

_____

_____

_____

_____

_____

_____

Things we made in class

My Favorite Artwork

The most challenging thing I did was.........

_____

_____

_____

_____

I appreciate you.......... **THANK YOU**

_____

_____

_____

I always looked forward to..........

_____

_____

_____

I would tell new students in your class next year......

 Drawing

I would like to say.............

_____
_____
_____
_____
_____
_____
_____
_____
_____
_____
_____

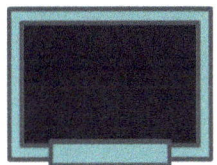

A drawing of our classroom......

I wish you a good holiday because..........

_____

_____

_____

_____

_____

_____

_____

Our School

It was funny when..................

_____

_____

_____

_____

_____

Something that surprised me............

_____

_____

_____

_____

 # Kindness

📋 You taught me to ....

_____

_____

_____

_____

Something that I will never forget is.............

_____

_____

_____

_____

Thank you

My Teacher's Pages

My Favorite time of the School Day............

_____

_____

_____

Something I learned this year.............

_____

_____

_____

 A class memory to Cherish...........

I will miss............

Teacher Keepsakes

One Hundred Years From Now

(excerpt from within my power by Forest Witcraft)

It will not matter
what kind of car I drove
what kind of house I lived in,
how much money was in my bank account
nor what my clothes looked like.
But the world may be a better place because
I was important in the life of a child

www.ingramcontent.com/pod-product-compliance
Lightning Source LLC
LaVergne TN
LVHW071340181025
823786LV00062B/2325